RIDING WESTERN

ALLEN RIDER GUIDES

Riding Western

Jane Lake

Foreword by Marjorie Barr

J. A. Allen

London

British Library Cataloguing in Publication Data

Lake, Jane
Riding Western.
1. Western riding
I. Title
798.2'3'0978   SF309.3

ISBN 0–85131–432–5

Published in Great Britain by
J. A. Allen & Company Limited,
1, Lower Grosvenor Place, Buckingham Palace Road,
London, SW1W 0EL

Book production Bill Ireson

Printed in Great Britain by W.B.C. Print Ltd, Bristol

Foreword

Jane Lake satisfies, in my view, the three requisites needed for a book such as this. She has been involved in Western riding and its small enthusiastic world, for 16 years; she has an acute interest in and a sense of the history of this form of horsemanship and of all that it comprises. Finally, most important of all, she can write. Those who read horse books will have discovered too often that the author may be marvellous over fences or in the dressage arena – but quite incapable of passing across their knowledge in print. Jane Lake suffers from no such handicap.

In *Riding Western* the author makes a contribution that will be enjoyable and useful to all Western riders and indeed to anyone with a broad interest in horsemanship.

I was born in Nebraska and brought up on a stock farm, so have ridden Western all my life. I hope this justifies my accepting the pleasant task of writing this introduction.

MARJORIE BARR
President, Western Horsemen's Association of Great Britain

Contents

List of Illustrations

List of Abbreviations

As the power and influence of Spain spread throughout the Americas, during and after the time of the Conquistadores, so Spanish came to influence and eventually dominate the language of the stock raising and ranching community of the continent.

In the text, I have indicated the origin of some of the more common words in use in Western riding by use of the following abbreviations.

Am.	=	American
Sp.	=	Spanish
S. Am. Sp.	=	South American Spanish
Mex.	=	Mexican
C. Am. Sp.	=	Central American Spanish
Chi.	=	Chilean
Ec.	=	Ecuadorian

Introduction

There have been many excellent books written on the breaking and training of the Western horse and the training of the Western rider. This book does not set out to be the definitive work on Western riding, but to outline the skills of both Western horse and rider, and to explain how the fascinating history of this form of riding still influences its modern counterpart.

1 A Short History of Western Riding

The horse, to lovers of the Western film genre, may be simply the mode of transport by which their heroes get from A to B, but in the not-so-romantic reality of the American West, it was the horse who was the hero, the essential hub of life in nineteenth-century Western America.

The cinema also does little to depict the true art of Western riding; a style developed from the Spanish school and which does, therefore, share the same roots as the better-known 'Classical' style. To fully understand Western riding and all it encompasses, it is necessary to know a little of its history.

When the Spanish Conquistadores landed in the New World in the sixteenth century, their horses were the first to set hoof on the land since their equine forbears, once native to the American continent, had died out about 9,500 years before. The blood of these Spanish mounts dominated American equine culture for many years until it was crossed with other European breeds, imported via the east coast of the United States.

The Spaniards brought with them not only their horses but their training methods and knowledge of open-range husbandry which were to become the blue-prints for the American ranching industry and the Western riding style. The early Western Americans adopted and, to a degree, adapted the Spanish methods and language to suit their needs. Today, Western riding carries the indelible stamp of the Spanish culture and tongue. Thus the riding style of the American cowboy developed making easy the job of stock raising in open country. Western riding has a good reason for everything connected with it; from training methods, equipment and tack to the clothing of the riders.

Many people still earn their living from the back of a stock horse, while others prefer to follow the amateur and professional rodeo (S. Am. Sp. *rodear* = to round up) and show circuits. Many more choose this form of riding purely for the pleasure of riding the trails and enjoying equine companionship. Western riding is now popular in several countries around the world, and, it is hoped, it is a riding form even more people will come to experience, study and, most importantly, enjoy.

2 The Western Horse

A good Western horse should possess the qualities of versatility, stamina, agility and balance; the horse's agility being aided by a small stature. The average height should be about 15 h.h.

The true 'Western' horse is descended from the mounts of the New World conquerors; horses that were of predominantly Barb blood. The Spanish had, in turn, inherited this breed from their conquerors, the Moors.

When the Iberian gold-seekers reached the southern border of what is now the United States, parties moved west and east. The offspring of the horses that travelled west became known as mustangs (Mex. *mesteño* = wild, untamed), and those of the eastern explorers' horses, Chickasaw ponies. The Chickasaws were an eastern Indian tribe.

The American Quarter Horse is, perhaps, the classic example of the Western type. The first Quarter Horses were bred in the 1700s by the fusion of Thoroughbred and Chickasaw blood in the eastern states. They became known as Quarter Running horses (which was soon shortened to Quarter horses) when they proved unbeatable in a quarter of a mile race.

Despite this ability they were not pampered racehorses, but were expected to put in a hard day's work pulling wagons and farm implements and as saddle horses. This, together with a life out in all weathers and rough feed, moulded the horses into a tough, sturdy breed.

When the long trek west began, the pioneers took their horses with them, and when they bred their horses with the Spanish stock of the south-western ranching community, the horses acquired another valuable asset; the ability to handle cattle.

In recent years more cross-breeding with the Thoroughbred

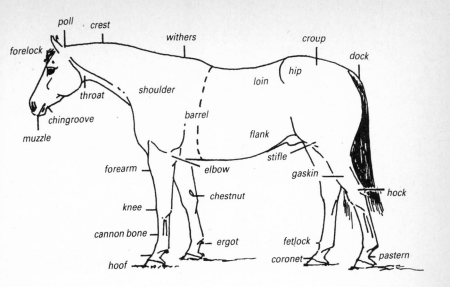

Points of a horse

has produced a finer, speedier horse for the racetrack and show ring, a move some Quarter Horse purists do not endorse.

Today, not all horses used in the Western field can boast about their Spanish ancestors, but they all share the trait of versatility; breeds such as the Arab, Appaloosa and the Morgan Horse. This quality of versatility is found in many breeds all over the world which makes it easier for non-American riders to choose mounts. Most breeds can be schooled to 'go Western', and in England some of the native breeds, or native crosses, make good Western horses. Indeed, the British Western horses should be applauded for displaying their versatility so ably. They are expected to cope with all Western events and not specialise in any one event as do many of the American show horses. As with all horse sports, however, the rider must choose an animal to suit his own ability and requirements.

As more and more people today buy horses for pleasure riding or showing, the modern Western horses may never see a cow, other than in the neighbouring field, and it is, therefore, very important to remember the roots of Western riding.

Western riding is a working form of riding and the Western horse is, in truth, simply a tool to get a job done, albeit a hard-working and companionable tool. The slightly stylised events of the Western show ring are designed to show off skills that a working horse would use every day, as the rodeo enables the cowboy to demonstrate his, and his horse's, craft.

The stock horse is the equine equivalent of the sheep dog, driving cattle and flushing them from places from which they have no desire to be flushed! A good stock horse should almost be able to work cattle without a guiding hand on the reins. Their work is broken down into two main categories: cutting and roping.

It is the cutting horse who really shows how well-developed this 'cow savvy', or knowledge of the bovine mind, is. The cowboy must guide his horse into the herd without upsetting them, point him in the direction of the chosen cow, cut it out

The cutting horse

from the herd (hence cutting horse) and keep it away from the herd until it can be roped and branded or given veterinary treatment. Simple as this may sound, it takes a great deal of hard work, agility and anticipation of the moves a cow is likely to make, to keep it away from the herd where it feels safe.

Once the cow has been cut out from the herd, the cowboy on the roping horse takes over. He must rope the cow, then tying or dallying the rope round the saddle horn, he dismounts and ties the cow's feet together so that it can be treated. It is the rope horse's job, once his rider has dismounted to attend to the cow, to keep the rope taut to ensure that the animal on the other end of the rope remains as immobile as possible. A slack rope gives the cow freedom to move which could be dangerous for man and horse. Should the cow move towards him, the horse is trained to back away to keep the rope taut; if the cow tries to run away from the horse before its feet are tied, then the horse sits back on his haunches to brace himself against the pull and stop the cow.

These skills are demonstrated in the rodeo arena by the calf and steer roping and cattle cutting contests. Many horses will do both jobs, but, more often than not, a horse will show a talent for one or the other.

When a horse works cattle his agility helps him to make certain moves which keep the cattle where he wants them – movements such as turning suddenly, swinging round and moving off again in the direction from which he came or moving forward fast from a standstill and stopping suddenly. Although the old-time cowboys and their mounts executed these movements without being aware of doing anything out of the ordinary, the movements have, today, been given names such as pivots, rollbacks, spins and sliding stops. These, together with reining back, changing leads, flying changes of leads and circles, are all everyday movements to the cow horse. In the show ring, they are all grouped together and tested in reining pattern classes.

One thing that helps make a top Western horse is good balance. He works with light contact on his mouth and fairly long reins, and this freedom enables him to use his head and neck to balance his own weight (in the same way that the beaver and kangaroo use their tails for balance) and that of his rider. The ideal head carriage is one where the horse's eyes are on a

The roping horse

level with his withers (at the base of the neck); too high or too low a head carriage will unbalance the horse.

To work well the horse must also be collected with his hindlegs under his body so that he is driven by the impulsion of the hindlegs. He is not collected to the degree of a horse schooled in the Classical style, but a well balanced, collected Western horse is able to obey a command to execute a movement promptly and, it is hoped, fruitfully.

The paces of the Western horse enable him to cover ground as tirelessly and comfortably as possible. A horse that worked all day and then had to double as a taxi as well, would not have lasted long if made to gallop everywhere; galloping was a pace reserved for short spurts when working cattle or in an emergency.

The walk, jog and lope are the three Western paces. The jog is a slow trot and the lope a slow canter. Both these paces are executed close to the ground as a horse with a high exaggerated action would tire easily and be less comfortable for the rider. The exception to this rule is the Morgan horse breed which is divided into two sections: the 'Park' and 'Pleasure' horses. The 'Park' type has a very high-stepping action, but the 'Pleasure' Morgans with a slightly lower action are comfortable to ride and favoured by many as stock horses.

3 Western Tack and its Uses

Western tack differs in style and application from English tack, but the basic rules of fitting, to ensure comfort for the horse, are the same.

The Western saddle is the youngest member of a family tree whose roots were formed by the war saddles of the Middle Ages and, in time, the seeds of the modern stock saddle were carried into the New World by the Conquistadores. The most 'modern' innovation, other than the recent idea of special saddles for special jobs, is the saddle horn. This put in its first appearance in the early-nineteenth ceutury. The Spanish Spade bit, which is still used today, and the bosal are also heirlooms from the Conquistadores.

Western tack ranges from the plain and workmanlike to the highly tooled, carved and silver-adorned saddles and bridles popular for parades and the show ring.

The Bit

The subject of bits and bitting is a highly complicated, and sometimes controversial, one; every rider and trainer having their own thoughts and ideas on the matter, but the first priority is that the bit fits and suits the horse.

The bit is the instrument that helps to gain maximum control over the speed and direction of the horse and, combined with the bridle, works on certain areas of the horse's head to achieve, not only control, but the correct carriage and balance of the horse. When the Western bit is brought into play, the action applied should be give and take; no request should be made with continuous pressure on the mouth.

To enable the Western horse to do his job efficiently, the bits are designed to get a quick response but to keep the animal light-mouthed.

Western bits are divided into two main categories; the ringed snaffles and the shanked bits. There are a number of variations on a theme within these categories which may be gentle or severe in their action. The snaffles exert gentle pressure directly on the mouth and the shanked bits combined with a varying degree of port (the metal of many curb bit mouthpieces is curved upward to form a low, medium or high port) and a curb strap or chain, give more leverage i.e. pressure on the mouth, tongue and into the curb (chin) groove via the cheek shanks. The longer the shanks of a bit the greater the leverage and control.

The Western, or shanked, snaffle is really a misnomer; the bit does not work like a snaffle, but employs the action of a shanked bit.

The Californian (Spanish) Spade bit and its offspring the half-breed are often thought to be cruel, but they were designed by men who were experts at training horses, and, with good handling, these bits encourage a lightness of mouth and movement in the horse which can only be obtained from a horse at ease with its work and suffering no discomfort. The very high port of the Spade bits enables the horse to feel the slightest movement of the bit against the roof of the mouth and respond to this. These bits often have copper on the mouthpiece which encourages a horse to salivate and, many say, a moist mouth is a light mouth. All good Spades have a roller or cricket on the mouthpiece which the horse can play with; this quiets the animal and, again, encourages salivation.

Quite often the modern Spades have 'loose jawed' shanks to the bit i.e. they are not solidly fixed to the mouthpiece; this enables the horse to feel the cue, or instruction, from the movement of the shanks before the mouthpiece moves.

The Half-Breed bit is a modification of the Spade bit.

It must be remembered that the design of a bit can make it potentially severe, but only if it is mishandled by the rider. Even the mildest of bits can be severe in the wrong hands, and continued abuse of a bit can result in a horse with a permanently damaged mouth and/or jaw.

Some Western trainers like to start their young horses in a

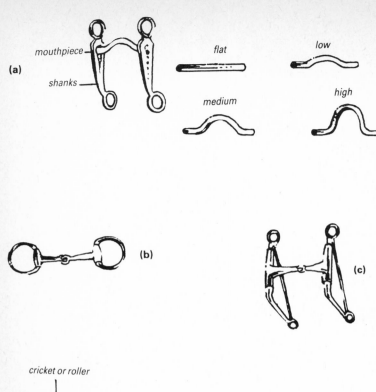

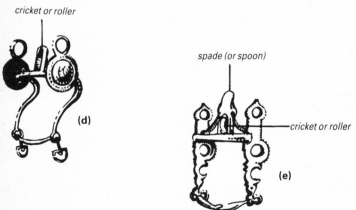

Bits: **(a)** Curb bit with mouthpieces showing varying degree of port; **(b)** Eggbutt snaffle with jointed mouthpiece; **(c)** Western, or shanked 'snaffle'; **(d)** Half-breed bit; **(e)** Spanish Spade bit

snaffle and then bring them on to a curb or Spade bit. Others may go from snaffle to hackamore to curb, and yet others may start a horse in a hackamore and work him up to the curb or Spade perhaps going via the snaffle.

Different trainers, different methods; some leave their horses in a snaffle, and there are now classes in some Western shows catering specifically for snaffle-bitted horses, but there are many other trainers who believe that a Western horse is not 'finished' until he's working in a curb bit.

FITTING THE BIT AND BRIDLE Every horse has a different sized mouth and needs a different width of bit. Too wide a bit will slide from side to side in the horse's mouth, and too narrow a bit will pinch the mouth. The bit should rest on the toothless bars of the mouth, and when in the correct position should just wrinkle the corners of the horse's mouth, but should not pull the corners of the mouth up.

A curb chain must be twisted until all the links are flat before being hooked up, and both a curb chain or strap must be loose enough so that it only causes pressure in the curb groove when contact is made with the reins. When the rein pull has been relaxed, so should the pressure in the curb groove.

The browband of the bridle must also be relatively loose around the horse's forehead so that it does not pull the crown piece against the back of the horse's ears and cause chafing, or pull the cheek pieces too close to the eyes.

The throatlash is employed to keep the bridle in place but must not be buckled tightly into the horse's throat area where the head joins the neck, or it may cause breathing problems and pinch the skin when the horse flexes his neck. A gap of four fingers width between the throat lash and the throat is a good guide.

BRIDLES Western bridles can be made of flat or rounded leather, the latter making excellent show bridles. Many Western bridles leave the horse's head totally uncluttered, and although browbands may be used to help keep the bridle in place, nosebands (other than the hackamores) are rarely seen unless a tie-down (the Western martingale) is used.

The split-ear or one-ear bridle does not have a noseband or a

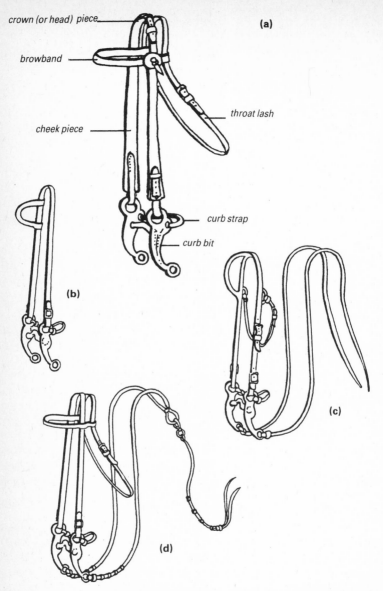

Western bridles: **(a)** Parts of the bridle; **(b)** One-ear headstall without throatlash; **(c)** Split-ear bridle with split reins; **(d)** Bridle with Californian style joined reins plus romal with a browband and loose throatlash

browband, but the crown, or head, piece has a split or loop on one side through which the horse's ear on the same side is pulled. This secures the bridle well enough for even the throatlash to be made redundant.

The split-ear was a popular bridle with the old-time cowboys because it could be easily repaired or replaced with a strip of leather or a belt (should the cowboy be wearing one!). A knife split was made in the leather and the horse's ear pulled through.

For further simplicity and ease of repair many bridles were (and some still are) laced with leather thonging at the points where the bridles and reins joined the bit, thus ensuring that, should the bridle break whilst the cowboy was in the middle of nowhere, it could be repaired with spare strips of leather or a saddle string – a problem not so easily remedied with broken buckles.

REINS   Western reins can be anything up to 2 m (7 ft) in length and are either split or joined. The Californian joined reins have a length of leather, the romal (Sp. *ramal* = strand [of a rope] halter, or, off-shoot), at the end which may be used as a quirt (S. Am. Sp. *cuarto* = whip, riding crop).

THE HACKAMORE   The hackamore (S. Am. Sp. *jaquima* = headstall), like many of the potentially severe bits should only be used by riders with experience and an understanding of how these things work, otherwise considerable damage can be done to the horse.

The hackamore is a bitless bridle which acts on the soft, lower part of the nose; pressure on this sensitive part can give as much control as a bit. Hackamore training takes about six months and in this time a young horse can be working cattle and learning this, or any other, job while being brought on to a bit slowly, thus ensuring a light undamaged mouth.

With all hackamores the action must be 'pull and release', give and take. Continuous pulling gives continuous pressure on the nose and kills the nerves in this area in the same way that continuous pulling on a bit deadens the nerves of the mouth.

THE BOSAL   The bosal (Sp. *bozal* = muzzle; S. Am. Sp. = halter, headstall) is the original Spanish hackamore favoured by

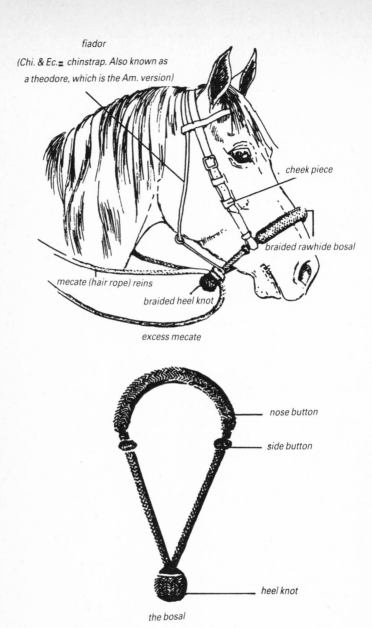

fiador
*(Chi. & Ec.= chinstrap. Also known as
a theodore, which is the Am. version)*

cheek piece

braided rawhide bosal

mecate (hair rope) reins

braided heel knot

excess mecate

nose button

side button

heel knot

the bosal

The original Spanish hackamore or bosal

the Mexicans and Californians. It acts on the nose and the nerves of the jaw. It is a braided rawhide noseband, attached to a headstall, which tapers into a braided heel knot. The mecate (Mex. = fibre; Am. = McCarty) or hair rope reins are made from one length of rope. The reins attach directly to the heel knot by wrapping loops of the rope round the knot; the loose end is then threaded through the bosal and is tied to the saddle. The loose end can be used as a lead rope, and, to ensure that the bosal fits the horse correctly, it can be used to make extra wraps around the heel knot to make it smaller, or unwrapped to make it larger. This increase or decrease of the wraps also increases or lessens the pressure as required by any one horse.

The positioning of the bosal on the nose is also very important; if it is too high it will not have much effect, and if it is too low it can cut off the horse's wind.

A bosal is often used in conjunction with a bit to form a type of double bridle to introduce a horse to the bit and bit control slowly.

THE MECHANICAL HACKAMORE This has the shanked cheeks of a bit but no mouthpiece. The shanks are attached to a stout noseband and a curb strap. When the reins are pulled, the leverage action causes pressure on the nose and in the chin groove, but none in the mouth.

Riders who wish to 'go Western' should remember that, by putting a Western curb, or curb-type, bit into the mouth of a horse who is used to a snaffle or other bit, or a hackamore round its nose, they cannot expect instant acceptance and understanding. Success comes with knowledge and patience; it takes time for a horse to learn and become 'finished'. There is an ultimate epithet for this highly trained and learned horse; he is said to be 'straight up' in the bridle.

Western saddles

Critics of the Western saddle say that it is very heavy. Heavier than the average Classical saddle it may be, but it is constructed to straddle the horse's back in the most comfortable way, and the combined weight of saddle and rider is evenly distributed over a large area of the horse's back. The design of the saddle also, to a degree, dictates the rider's position in the saddle, keeping them in one place so the lack of excessive movement puts less strain on the horse's back.

FITTING   Western saddles are used with a pad and/or blanket which help to spread the weight and absorb the sweat. Naturally, it is also very important that the saddle fits the horse correctly. Different breeds and types of horses have different conformations, and these differences must be taken into account when fitting a saddle. Saddles are now designed with varying tree structures to suit these differing conformations. Should it be

Western saddles: Californian, or round, skirt saddle, single-rigged. Near (left) side view

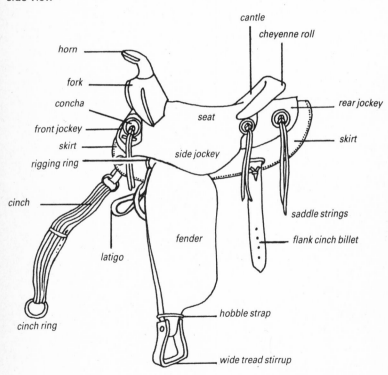

necessary, however, it is relatively easy to make a Western saddle fit most horses by judicious use of pads and blankets, but, in the long run, there is no substitute for a correctly fitting saddle.

The saddle must be clear of the withers at all times with no less than two fingers width between the withers and the gullet of the saddle *when the rider is in the saddle*; the rider's weight makes the saddle sit lower on the horse's back. If the tree structure is too wide for the horse the saddle will bear down on the withers and spine, and if it is too narrow the saddle will cause pinching and pressure.

Another Western saddle: Texan, or square, skirt saddle, double-rigged. Off (right) side view

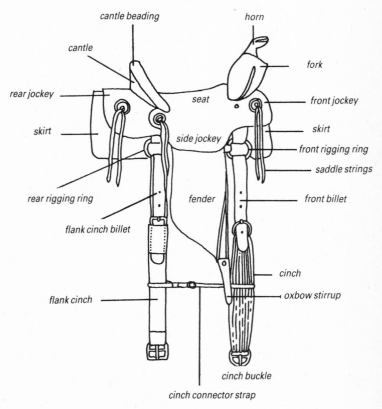

cantle beading

horn

cantle

fork

rear jockey

seat

front jockey

skirt

skirt

side jockey

front rigging ring

saddle strings

rear rigging ring

fender

front billet

flank cinch billet

cinch

flank cinch

oxbow stirrup

cinch buckle

cinch connector strap

29

When the saddle is in place it is advisable to lift the pad and blankets up into the gullet to provide an air passage and to stop the pads and blankets leaning on the withers. Even soft pads and blankets can cause pressure sores on the withers.

Whilst thinking about the fitting of the saddle, the rider's comfort should also be taken into consideration. Too long a seat for a small person may make them feel lost in the saddle, and too short a seat for a large person will be equally uncomfortable!

Many modern saddles have too severe a sloping seat which throws the rider to the back of the saddle and makes it impossible to maintain the correct position; the rider always being a little behind the forward movement of the horse. The flatter the seat the better.

A rider also has the choice of plain leather seats or padded seats, and, although padding may seem like an unnecessary luxury, many slim people I know who possess little padding of their own do find a little extra padding a boon!

First time Western saddle buyers sometimes make the mistake of buying a pony-sized Western saddle because, in comparison to an English, or Classical, saddle they can still look quite large. It is, therefore, advisable to look at a number of saddles and, if possible, fit them on the horse and try them out. A saddle that fits both horse and rider will contribute greatly to many hours of pleasurable and safe riding.

TYPES All Western saddles look alike until examined more closely, and types and designs differ to suit different usage. The two main divisions are:

1) The Cutting saddle. When the cutting horse makes his swift moves and changes of direction, the rider needs to be as secure and deep in the saddle as possible, therefore the forks of cutting saddles have wide swells spreading out from the pommel just below the horn. This added bulk helps to anchor the rider into the saddle, and undercut swells give even more security.

2) The Roping saddle. The men who rope the cattle need room to move, often stand up in the stirrups to rope, and have to dismount frequently to tend the cattle. This freedom is acquired by using a saddle that has no swells or very narrow

swells. The slick fork, or 'A' fork, saddles have no swells at all and give the most freedom.

Saddle horns vary in height and width, and cantles vary in height and dish (the inner curve of the cantle); some have simple cantle beading, others a Cheyenne roll, and saddle skirts may be rounded (Californian) or square (Texan). Again, these variations are not purely decorative.

A rider who does mainly cutting work does not need a tall horn and would favour a high cantle to aid a deep seat. The roper needs a tall horn around which to dally or tie his rope and a low cantle for ease of quick dismounting. Ropers also prefer a Cheyenne roll which may prevent the spurs getting hung up on the saddle when dismounting. The larger square skirts may add a little weight to a saddle, but they distribute the weight more evenly than the smaller, lighter rounded skirts. Square skirts can, however, sometimes chafe or rub a short-backed horse, such as the Arab, on the flanks.

STRUCTURE   Every saddle, no matter what its design or job, has a skeleton, or tree, around which it is built. Western trees are usually made of a hardwood or glass fibre bound with rawhide or bullhide.

A good Western saddle has the outer leather layers laced on to the tree by the saddle strings (those dangly leather things that most people think are for decoration!), and a quick guide to see whether or not this has been done, is to turn the saddle upside down when it should be possible to see or feel the leather lacing where it has gone through the sheepskin under-lining of the saddle. On the surface the saddle strings are used for tying items of equipment or clothing onto the saddle. Other good modern saddles have some saddle strings replaced with screw and ferrule fittings which anchor the leather layers to the tree equally securely. A cheaper saddle may simply have the outer layers stapled or nailed to the tree.

RIGGING   The cinch (Sp. *cincha* = girth) attaches to the rigging to keep the saddle in place. Rigging is either on-tree or in-skirt, i.e. the ring to which the cinch is attached is either in the leather rigging straps on the tree itself, or built into the skirt.

The cinch is fastened and tightened by a long leather strap called the latigo (Sp. = whip, lash) which is secured by either a buckle or is tied in a knot not unlike that of the old school tie!

RIGGING POSITIONS Over the years the rigging positions changed to suit the different methods of roping, and, more recently, selective breeding changed the conformation of the stock horse so the rigging positions had to alter to suit the changing equine shape.

When roping, the rider's weight should be kept over the centre of balance to help the horse do his job with the least strain. Ropers use a double-rigged saddle, that is, a saddle with the front cinch in the Spanish (rim-fire or full), $7/8$ or $3/4$ positions, plus a back or flank cinch to prevent the saddle tipping up behind when the weight of an animal on the end of the rope pulls on the saddle horn.

The above three rigging positions may be single- (without a flank cinch) or double- (with a flank cinch) rigged, but the $5/8$ and centre-fire rigs are always single-rigged.

Pleasure riders can choose whichever rigging they prefer, but saddles with the $3/4$ and $7/8$ rigging place the rider over the horse's centre of balance and give both rider and horse a comfortable ride.

As Western show events and the rodeo became more specialised and competitive, saddle makers rose to the occasion and designed and made saddles to fit a particular job; the two categories of cutting and roping saddles are not now enough to cover demand.

For the pleasure riders mentioned above, a saddle has been made with a structure that allows the rider to use it for any number of events. It will serve them well in the ring should they choose to enter a show, but will also be comfortable for trail riding. It is the Western equivalent of the general purpose saddle.

Lightweight saddles are made for Barrel Racing and other speed events, and for Endurance Riding when a horse covering long distances, within a time limit and often over rough ground, needs all the help he can get.

The Professional Rodeo Cowboys Association now states that all saddle-bronc riders have to use an Association saddle which

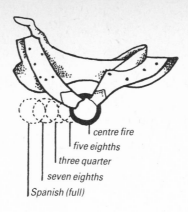

centre fire
five eighths
three quarter
seven eighths
Spanish (full)

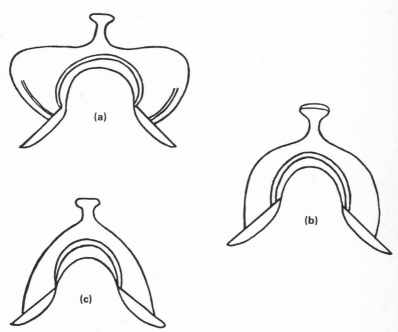

(a)

(b)

(c)

Five saddle rigging positions *(top)*. Saddle forks: **(a)** The swell-fork saddle. Saddles with these wide swells help to keep a rider in the saddle. Cutting saddles have these wide swells; **(b)** The narrow-fork saddle. Narrow swells have a little anchorage, but are narrow enough not to hinder a rider who needs freedom in a roping saddle; **(c)** The slick, or 'A', fork saddle. The lack of any swells on this saddle gives the most freedom to a rider, like a roper, who needs to mount and dismount frequently

gives all competitors an equal chance of winning, or not, depending on the rider's ability! This saddle came into being when, several years ago, cowboys were coming up with every trick in the book to keep themselves in the saddle when riding bucking horses; the contests were battles of ingenuity rather than riding skill.

Western saddles are expensive and British Western riders are advised to pick the best saddle they can afford which is comfortable for both horse and rider. If in doubt about the best style and fit, riders should seek the advice of someone who knows what to look for. The horse, at least, will be grateful for this advice!

Stirrups

The wide, wooden Western stirrups are designed for comfort and safety. They can be of plain wood or bound in leather or have a leather tread, and others may have the leather tapaderos (Sp. *tapadera* = lid or cover), the hooded covers to protect the feet from brush country and the elements. Children's saddles are often with covers, or tapaderos, on the stirrups to prevent small feet slipping right through the stirrups. Some covered stirrups are also used by the Riding for the Disabled Association for the same safety reasons.

The wider and heavier the stirrup the easier it is to pick it up and quit it when mounting and dismounting, and it is difficult for a foot to get hung up in a wider stirrup should the rider fall.

The narrower oxbow stirrup fits neatly into the instep for those such as cutting horse riders, barrel racers and bronc riders who do not wish to leave the saddle quite so often as the ropers! It is, therefore, a secure but not quite such a safe stirrup. The fender, or sudadero (Sp. *sudar* = to sweat, to ooze) protects the leg from being rubbed by the stirrup leather beneath it, and keeps the horse's sweat off the leg.

The Rope

The rope was the one essential tool the old-time cowboy could not do without. At the time there were no fences to stop the cattle running from Texas to the Canadian border and if he needed several throws to catch an animal, then he would have been better off hanging up his hat and saddle and taking a job as a bank clerk!

Cowboys working in brush and cactus country used a short rope or reata (S. Am. Sp. *la reata* = lariat), about 9 m (30 ft) long, to prevent getting the rope caught up in the spiky bushes, but cowboys working in the brush-free plains country used a long rope of about 18 m (60 ft).

Two styles of roping developed. There were those, like the Texans, who believed in tying their ropes 'hard and fast' to the saddle horn, and those who preferred to dally (Sp. *dar la vuelta* = to take a turn), or wrap, the rope round the horn. Whichever method was used, it was a skilled job, and the ropes, like all Western equipment, changed and improved to make the job a little easier. Braided rawhide was tough and light to handle but could be temperamental in bad weather. Ropes made of grass and plant fibres, such as hemp, sisal, maguey and manila, proved to be cheaper and more durable than rawhide.

The modern working cowboy has science on his side, and ropes are made of man-made fibres such as nylon. These modern fibres keep the ropes kink free and easy to coil in all weathers.

Spurs

The familiar picture of a Western spur is of finely-honed points on the end of a rowelled spur the size of a cartwheel. However, the modern Western spur has smaller rowels and the points are blunted. Because the rowel is free moving it tends to roll down the horse's side rather than sticking straight in like a solid spur.

The art of wearing any spur is knowing when and how to use it, and to be able to use the leg without the spur making contact if it is not required. If in doubt, don't use them!

Western work spur: the Western spur is held in place by a leather strap over the instep, but rarely has a strap under the instep

35

Spurs are an extra artificial aid and should be used solely for a turn of speed in emergencies, or to encourage a lethargic horse when one light touch of the spurs may produce a better result than perpetual kicking.

4 Training

There are two schools of Western training and riding; the Californian and the Texan, and although the methods, equipment and riding styles vary slightly, people adapt them to their own requirements and the ultimate result is the same.

In the heyday of the cattle industry many of the big ranchers had on the payroll a man who was employed solely to break-in the ranch horses. Smaller ranches employed a freelance horse breaker who went from ranch to ranch to do the same job.

This man worked alone to get a large number of range-wild horses broken-in enough for the cowboys to take them over, and he usually worked to a tight schedule. It is not surprising, therefore, that most of the horses barely had the rough edges knocked off them or that horse-breakers were old men with battered bodies by the time they were 35. The horses were handed over to the cowboys having only just got used to a saddle, bridle and rider, and the cowboys accepted their green-broke horses stoically, expecting to have to ride the bed springs out of them every morning!

The novice cow horses learned their work by being 'thrown in the deep end' with the cattle on the open range.

Today, the early training of a young Western horse differs little from the training of other young horses, and the modern trainers have more time to spend with them. The horse will benefit from early handling, patience with firmness and school work. Acceptance of the bridle and bit, or hackamore, saddle and rider is essential, but he must also learn to acquire the Western qualities of agility, versatility and stamina, plus be alert and obedient. An alert stock horse can save his rider a good deal of time and energy. It is hoped that a horse is born with some, if not all, of these qualities, but good training, feeding and care will help a horse develop and perform to the best of his ability, and keep him fit and happy.

The school work helps the horse to become the complete athlete. The horse must work equally well on both the left and right rein (i.e. moving in both directions), and is worked in circles, serpentines (a series of loops across the school) and figures-of-eight at all paces.

These exercises teach the horse to flex his head, neck and spine ensuring a suppleness and coordination of the whole body which enables the horse to work efficiently and well.

In the course of his work, the Western horse will have to move sideways and backwards as well as forwards and much of the Western training includes work most people associate with dressage; movements such as leg-yielding, side-passing and reining-back (backing-up). To complete his training the horse must progress to pivots, rollbacks, flying changes of leads etc.

To compare the training of the Western horse to dressage is perhaps to imply that modern Western training has been influenced by dressage. This is not so. Remember that both the Western and the Classical styles stem from the same roots, so dressage is not a new influence. The ultimate aim of dressage is to produce a supremely athletic, balanced and obedient horse. (It was used originally in war by cavalrymen whose lives could be saved by the quick moves and obedience of their mounts when fighting at close quarters.) The training of the Western horse has *always* had to produce these things otherwise the horse could not do his job successfully. The Western horse was, and in many cases still is, trained to earn his keep.

Neck-Reining

Many people associate Western riding with the one-handed neck-reining. Neck-reining is the opposite to direct-reining, or plough-reining, i.e. the horse moves away from pressure on his neck rather than being 'led' into a turn.

This method of reining leaves one hand free for roping or other work, or, as in the wars of the Middle Ages, to wield a sword! A right-handed rider ropes with the right hand and guides the horse with the left and vice versa. But, unless a rider is roping or competing in the showring it is *not wrong* to use two hands. Indeed, the majority of trainers work their young stock with two hands and introduce neck-reining later in their schooling.

To teach a horse to neck-rein it is best to apply a combination of direct-reining and neck-reining. The horse is asked to turn left with the direct left rein, and, simultaneously, the rider neck-reins to the left with the right rein and 'pushes' the horse over to the left with the right leg. Once the horse understands the feeling of pressure on the neck, he will learn to turn away from it, and the direct-reining can cease gradually. To neck-rein to the right the aids are reversed.

Backing-up

Backing or Reining-back is an important movement for the Western horse because he will come across a number of situations where backing-up is the only solution to a problem. As already mentioned, he may have to back to keep a rope taut, and there may be times when he does not have the space or time to move forward and turn in a circle, so back-up he must. Backing-up, however, is not an easy or natural manoeuvre for a horse and it must be taught with patience.

Firstly, the horse must be at the halt with his hocks underneath him. Even pressure with both legs asks for movement, but he is restricted from moving forward by applying even pressure with the reins (or alternatively applying one rein and then the other), employing the pull and release tactic. Once he realises that he is required to move but cannot go forward, he should take a step back. As soon as he does, all pressure must be relaxed and the horse rewarded. Then he may be asked again, increasing the distance backed gradually and steadily.

Should a horse have difficulties learning this lesson, it may help to have an assistant on the ground who, whilst the rider gives the aids from the saddle, taps (not hits) the horse on the chest or forelegs with a whip saying 'back'. The horse should then move away from the whip, and be rewarded as soon as he steps back.

It is good that the horse also learns the verbal cue 'back' as this makes it easier for a rider to have the command obeyed in situations when he is dismounted.

There are one or two training ideas which are essentially Western.

The Western horse has to tolerate a great many things, such as ropes whistling past his ear, hanging down from his saddle or dragging a weight behind him. He must learn not to kick when surrounded by milling cattle, and accept coats flapping round him when his rider puts one on or takes one off while in the saddle. He should not, therefore, be of a naturally spooky and unsteady nature.

One method some trainers use to acclimatise a horse to these things is sacking-out. This involves tying the horse firmly but safely with a short rope and a stout headcollar to a snubbing post or fence in a small paddock or corral (Sp. = yard, cattle pen). The trainer then takes a sack, blanket, or similar item, up to the horse and lets him sniff it. It is then rubbed gently all over his body and round and in between his legs. Once this has been accepted the sack can be applied more vigorously, building up to a point where the horse will accept it being waved all round his head, body and legs.

Although a cow horse must be as steady as possible, there is no method of spook-proofing that is 100 per cent reliable. Horses can, and will, be upset by things we cannot see, hear or feel; they see the world totally differently from us, and, consequently, there cannot be any such thing as a bomb-proof horse.

Ground-tying

A cowboy tending to cattle on foot cannot take the time to tie his horse to anything, even if there is anything in the neighbourhood to tie his horse to, and so a stock horse must learn to ground-tie. He is taught not to move when his reins are dropped on the ground, and the split reins of many Western bridles ensure that the horse cannot put his foot through them and damage himself or the bridle.

Teaching a horse to ground-tie is rather like teaching a dog to 'stay', and it is advisable to start this training in a well fenced area or the horse may be lost to greener pastures!

Once the rider has dismounted and the reins have been dropped on the ground, the horse is told to 'stand'. A light tug on the reins may be advantageous at this point, making the horse feel he is being checked and told to 'stand' by the reins and bit. As soon as the horse remains still, the rider moves away from the horse. Should the horse move, the rider must go back to the horse, repeat the command and move away again. The rider should be able to go further and further away, eventually moving out of sight, while the horse remains still.

If the horse is learning well, his rider must not then make the mistake of calling the horse to him, thereby allowing the horse to move. He must go to the horse and pick up the reins before allowing him to move, otherwise he has defeated the object of the lesson.

If a horse will not learn to ground-tie or has to be left for any length of time, or if joined reins are used, then hobbling could prove to be a better method of anchoring the horse.

Hobbling

Teaching a horse to accept hobbles also takes time and patience. Some horses fight them to begin with and need to be watched to ensure they don't damage themselves, but once the horse learns how to 'hop' with hobbles on, he can move freely although his speed is restricted.

Hobbles are fitted round the pasterns of the forelegs and should be adjusted so that they are not loose enough to slip and rub the horse's legs, or to allow the horse to pull his feet free, nor should they be too tight.

Jumping

The Western horse should be capable of jumping small, natural fences, such as fallen trees or ditches, that he may meet on the trail, and riders wishing to enter Trail classes should ensure that their horses do have this ability.

The Western saddle is not, however, designed for jumping big upright fences; the horn can do a great deal of damage to the anatomy of a rider adopting the forward seat required for these bigger fences!

Converting the 'English' horse

There is absolutely no reason why a horse cannot be ridden in both the English and Western styles, and many shows have a Versatility class in which the horses are judged working under both forms of tack.

Unless it is possible to buy a young horse and school it Western right from the start or buy a 'made' Western horse, then it is usually a matter of having to re-school an 'English' horse. This is not a case of just sticking a Western saddle on his back, a Western bit in his mouth, dressing up in all the right gear and expecting miracles; it takes a little time and patience.

The first thing that will seem strange to the horse is having less contact with the mouth; lessening contact with the 'English' horse may have been an invitation to pick up speed, but the Western horse must go faster only when the leg aids tell him to do so. Neither is the looser rein an invitation to him to drift along with his nose between his knees and all the weight on the forehand; the forward drive of the budding Western horse must still come from the hindquarters. He must learn to balance himself without the help of the strong mouth contact, and develop a natural but not over-bent head carriage.

The next change for the horse, will be to drop the speed of his paces down a gear to the close-to-the-ground smoother gaits.

'English' horses used to walking with close contact are given a long, loose rein as a reward and relaxation after work well done. The Western horse must walk on a loose rein maintaining the animation and impulsion of a good walk.

Once the horse is walking well on the lighter contact, he can be asked to trot. By gently checking with the reins an attempt must be made to reduce the trot to a jog, and in order to prevent the horse slowing to a walk, light leg pressure is maintained to keep him moving.

The same technique must be applied to reduce the canter to a lope. When the horse is moving well and comfortably at the canter and on the correct lead, check with the reins to reduce the canter to a lope, and, again, light leg pressure should be maintained to stop him coming back to the jog.

In all cases, as soon as the required pace is achieved, relax the hand and leg pressure.

It should, perhaps, be emphasised that although the Western horse works on a loose rein with light mouth contact, there *must be* a light contact; the reins must not be hanging in loops! The only people who may be forgiven for having the reins extremely slack are cutting horse riders, who, when in the show ring or rodeo arena, wish to show the judges that their horses are working on their own with little, or no, rein cues.

5 The Western Rider

The finest Spanish horsemen were masters of two riding styles. The first, known as *a la brida*, was a style used by the Christian crusaders in the Holy land; they rode with a very long stirrup and a heavily padded saddle with a high pommel and cantle. The second style, *a la gineta*, they learned from the Saracens who rode with very short stirrups and stood in the stirrups when riding at speed. The Spaniards derived a modification of the two styles which, in time, became the style of the cowboy and Western rider.

Because the Western and Classical styles of riding share the same beginnings, the instructions, aids or cues, that the rider must give and the horse respond to, are similar. Consequently a rider who has ridden in the Classical style should be able to adapt to the Western style in a comparatively short time, and a total novice who wishes to ride Western would come to no harm by learning the rudiments of riding at an English riding school. The natural aids of the hands, legs, seat, weight and voice are used in both riding styles as are the artificial aids, spurs and whips or quirts. The artificial aids should be used only as a last resort or in an emergency, and aids given by the hands, through the reins and the bit, must always be accompanied by the appropriate leg aids.

Tacking-up

Before a horse can be ridden he must have the saddle and bridle put on, and any rider worth the title (whether they own a horse or not) should be able to do this himself.

1) Stand by left side of horse's head.

2) Take off the headcollar and do up round the horse's head to stop him from walking away. (If the horse is not wearing a headcollar, put the reins round his neck so that you have some control.) Slip joined reins over the horse's head or lay split reins over the neck. (Split reins may be left hanging providing the ground is clean and dry!)

3) Place the right hand between the horse's ears and hold the crown, or head, piece, lifting the bridle so that the bit is level with the horse's mouth.

4) Slip the bit into the horse's mouth by holding the bit in the left hand and inserting the left thumb into the toothless corner of the mouth to encourage the horse to open his mouth. Hold the curb strap out of the way with the left little finger to ensure that this does not find its way into the horse's mouth with the bit! *Do not bang the bit against the horse's teeth.* This will not encourage him to open his mouth, but will make him head shy.

5) Once the bit is installed use the left hand to ease the horse's ears gently under the head piece, or to insert one ear through a split- or one-ear bridle.

6) If a curb chain is used, twist the chain until the links lie flat, then hook up.

7) If the bridle has a browband, pull the forelock over the top of it.

When trail riding, the bridle may be put on over the headcollar, and the lead rope may either be removed and tied to the saddle, or left on the headcollar with the lead rope coiled and tied securely to the saddle. When the horse has to be tied he can be secured by the lead rope with or without the bridle being removed. *A horse must never be tied by the reins.* Should he be frightened and pull back, his mouth can be severely damaged by the bit.

If, however, the horse has to be tied for any length of time it is best to remove the bridle, but if he is tied with the bridle on, make sure that joined reins are either looped over the saddle horn or tied to the saddle, and split reins can either be knotted and looped over the saddle horn or tied to the saddle. Make sure that the reins are not tied or looped so short that they are pulling on the horse's mouth, and that they are not so long that the horse can stand on them or put a foot through them.

SADDLING THE HORSE

1) Place the saddle pad and/or blanket well forward on the horse's lower neck and back, then slide them back onto the saddle area. This ensures that all his hairs are lying the right way.

2) Check to see that there is an equal amount of pad/blanket on either side of the horse.

3) Put the cinch and stirrups over the seat of the saddle (Western stirrups do not 'run-up' the stirrup leathers), so that they cannot bang against the horse, then, holding the gullet with the left hand and the saddle skirts (at rear) with the right hand, lift the saddle and place it gently on the horse's back.

4) Gripping the horn, give the saddle a gentle shake so that it slips into the correct place, then lift the saddle pad/blanket up into the gullet of the saddle.

5) Check the saddle on both sides to ensure that the saddle strings are not caught up and nothing is twisted or out of place.

6) Walking round to the off- (right) side, let the cinch down, then, returning to the near- (left) side, reach under the horse's stomach with the left hand, take hold of the cinch and check that it is not twisted. With the right hand feed the latigo strap through the cinch ring and tie or buckle to secure.

7) Just before mounting, tighten the cinch if necessary, and take down both stirrups from the seat. Check the cinch again after having ridden for about 10–15 minutes.

8) The cinch must be tight enough to secure the saddle, but must not 'cut the horse in half'. If a flank cinch is used it must be tightened just enough to allow it to do its job (i.e. to stop the back of the saddle tipping up), but must not be tight against the horse's belly not so loose that it will annoy the horse or let him catch a hind leg in it.

When saddling a horse for the first time, check that the tack fits properly.

Mounting

In my dim and distant youth, my riding instructor said that if you could mount a horse correctly you were one third of the way to learning to ride. A slight exaggeration perhaps, but it is surprising how many people (and not all novices) have trouble getting into the saddle.

Several years later, my first Western instructor watched me hippety-hopping about before launching myself saddleward, and when I eventually arrived said that I should dismount and try again. He then taught me a method I have found totally reliable ever since. His instructions were:

1) Check that the cinch is tight enough to stop the saddle from slipping.

2) Face the horse on the near-side.

3) Take the reins in the left hand, keeping them just short enough to prevent the horse from walking off when you are mounting, and place this hand on the horse's neck just in front of the withers.

4) Place the left foot in the stirrup taking care that the toe is not jabbing in the horse's side; point the toe down or towards the horse's head. Then, brace the left knee against the saddle and roll your weight onto the ball of the right foot.

5) With the right hand take hold of the saddle horn, the off-side swell, or place it on the off-side of the saddle. Do not hold the cantle because as you mount you pull the saddle towards you which can unbalance the horse.

6) Once balanced, swing the right leg over the saddle in one quiet, smooth movement, taking care not to knock the horse's rump on the way over.

7) Finally, settle quietly in the saddle (do not bump or collapse into it) and take up the right stirrup with the right foot.

Some people prefer to mount facing the rear of the horse as in the Classical style.

With practice, mounting in one fluid movement becomes easier, even for shorter-legged riders because, remember, that the average Western horse is not tall, and should not, therefore, present great mounting problems.

I also feel it is most important for a rider to be equally adept at mounting from the off-side, and for the horse to get used to this as well. Many's the time when out on the trail, that, because of difficult terrain, it is only possible to mount from the off-side, or the left stirrup leather may break forcing the rider to mount from the right.

Tradition is all very well, but there are not a great many people who wear swords today, so that swords cannot get in the way when mounting from the right!

Dismounting

1) Place the left hand, holding the reins, on the neck, and the right hand on the off-side swell or on the horn.
2) Take the right foot out of the stirrup, leaving the left foot in the stirrup.
3) Putting your weight into the left stirrup, swing the right leg clear of the rump and down to the ground.
4) Once the right foot touches the ground, remove the left foot from the stirrup.

Again, it is wise to practise dismounting on the off-side as well.

Riding Position

The Western riding position is, essentially, the same as that of the Classical style. The rider sits in the deepest part of the saddle without leaning forward or leaning back on the high cantle. The body should be relaxed (i.e. without tension, but not slouching) with a straight back, square shoulders, and with the rider's centre of balance over that of the horse. The leg is practically straight with just enough bend in the knee to allow a clearance of about 5 cm (2 in) between rider and saddle when standing in the stirrups.

A supple waist and knee and ankle joints act as shock absorbers to help the rider sit deep in the saddle at all paces. The ball of the foot rests on the stirrup and the toe should just be visible when looking down in a straight line from the knee. The heel should drop down, as this downward slant of the heel helps to 'pull' the rider's weight into the saddle. If the heel is allowed to come up, the rider's seat becomes insecure. The foot lies parallel to the horse, but it is not always considered a fault in Western riding if the toe turns out a little.

A good position in the saddle. Note the Californian reins coming up through the hand with the romal held in the other hand

Excessive turning out of the toe jeopardises a good leg position and seat.

It is important to develop an independent seat (i.e. one where the rider does not rely on the stirrups or hanging onto the reins or horn to keep them in the saddle), and to ride by balance. The knee and inner thigh should be in contact with the saddle, but riders must not grip with the knees; this tends to push the seat up and out of the saddle. The lower leg should lie close to the horse's side in readiness to give a cue as required, but, again, without gripping.

The body should be as still as possible; flapping arms and legs are unattractive and of no use to rider or horse, and an excessive rocking motion at the lope detracts from the quiet easy Western movement. The upper arm, from shoulder to elbow, remains close to the rider's side.

To achieve the perfect position is probably every rider's aim, but it is important to remember (and I feel some instructors should take note) that it is only possible to achieve as near a perfect position in the saddle as our physical make-up will allow.

The Hands

If novice riders work with two hands on the reins initially, it will help them keep their shoulders square, and if the body is correctly placed it becomes easier to find the balance. When riding one-handed every effort must be made to avoid letting the shoulder of the rein hand come forward, thus twisting the body and upsetting the balance of both rider and horse.

Whether riding with one or two hands, the hands must be kept low, light and remain still except when giving a little to the movement of the horse's head, or when giving a rein cue.

RIDING ONE-HANDED   The rein hand is kept low, just clearing the saddle horn, and, at this level, the hand may be held over the horn or just in front of it. As already mentioned, the Western horse works on a long rein with light contact, but the reins must not be so long that when they are brought into use, the rein hand is seen in the vicinity of the rider's ear before contact is made.

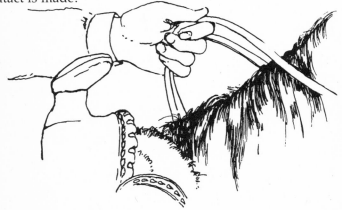

Split reins going down through the hand with fore finger inserted between them. The fore finger is never inserted between joined reins

The joined reins of the Californian bridle come up through the bottom of the hand and out over the index finger, and the romal is held in the other hand which rests on the thigh.

The split reins of the Texas style bridles pass either up through the hand or down through the hand and the excess length of rein is left to lie down the horse's shoulder, while the free hand rests on the thigh. If the reins come down through the hand the index finger may be inserted between them, or not, as the rider chooses.

Riders adopt the style that suits them best, but in the show ring definite rules are laid down, and riders are advised to find out what these are before entering the ring. It is, for instance, not 'good form' to change the reins from hand to hand in the ring.

Turning the Horse

To neck-rein a horse to the left, the left hand is pulled out to the left side, remaining on the same level as the normal hand position; the hand should not move up or back towards the body. As the hand moves, the right rein will come into contact with the horse's neck and he will turn away from the pressure.

These hand aids must be applied in conjunction with the correct leg aids. Whilst asking the horse to turn with the left hand, the right leg must apply a little pressure to 'push' the horse over to the left. The horse responds to the leg in the same way that he responds to the rein; he moves away from the pressure. When turning the horse to the right the hand and leg aids are reversed.

The Halt

With experience, a rider should be able to ask the horse for, and achieve, a halt from all paces, but this should not be confused with the sliding stop which is a movement requiring a good deal of experience and training.

To obtain a smooth halt, apply even pressure with the legs and ask the horse to stop with the reins. If he does not halt at once, release the pressure, then ask again (and again, if necessary) until he stops. Once he has halted do not let him move off again until he is told to.

The legs are applied to keep the horse's legs under him, so that he does not have to gather his hind end up first when asked to move on again or to back-up.

The Paces or Gaits

Cowboys were in the saddle for up to 18 hours a day, a fact that made comfort most important. The comfortable, fluid movements of the Western horse combined with the long stirrup enabled the rider to sit in the saddle at all paces.

THE WALK   The walk is a four-beat gait with one hoof off the ground at a time. The horse will move forward into a walk when light, even pressure is applied to his sides; the rider 'closes' his legs around the horse. The horse should stride out well in an animated fashion, and if he needs a reminder to maintain the pace, the legs should be closed on his sides again. The hand must give a little to the nodding movement of the horse's head.

THE JOG   The jog is a two-beat gait in which the legs move in diagonal pairs, i.e. near fore, off hind and off fore, near hind.

The Western rider does not rise (post) to the jog, but in some show classes where a slightly faster trot is called for, riders are allowed to rise.

To ask the horse to jog, apply even pressure with both legs, a little more firmly than when asking for the walk. Once the horse responds release the leg pressure.

It is the jog, and the slightly faster trot, that makes novices wonder why people ride horses for pleasure! It can be the least comfortable of the paces, but, with practise, a rider will get into the rhythm and it becomes easier to sit down into the saddle. The hand must be kept low, giving only to the movement of the horse's head.

THE LOPE   This slow canter is an extremely comfortable gait. It is a three-beat gait in which the horse leads with one or other of his forelegs.

When working in a school or in the show ring, it is important that the horse moves off into a lope on the correct leading leg which helps to keep the horse balanced when working on a circle. The leading leg is always the inside foreleg. It is not a bad idea to ask for a particular lead when riding in a straight line on the trail. This prevents the horse always picking his 'favourite' lead and becoming one-sided.

With a novice horse or rider it may be easier to teach the aids to the lope if two hands are used on the reins. The horse can be asked to lope from the jog or walk (or halt), but the novice rider will find it easier to achieve the pace from the jog and out of the corner of the school.

AIDS FOR A LEAD

(The aids described are for a left lead; those for a right lead are a reversal of the left lead.)

1) Take up a light contact with the horse's mouth.
2) Angle the horse's head slightly to the right with the right rein, keeping contact with the left rein to prevent the horse's body turning right.
3) Bring the outside leg (right leg) back and apply pressure behind the cinch whilst keeping the left leg on the cinch and placing a little weight in the left stirrup.
4) As soon as the horse strikes off in the left lead, relax leg and rein pressure, reapplying leg pressure if the horse attempts to come down to a jog before being requested to do so.

Turning a horse's head towards the outside of the circle encourages him to strike off with the inside leg, but once he becomes more experienced and used to the leg aids, he should strike off correctly with his head and neck bent in the direction he is going; an important factor when being ridden one-handed.

Again, practise will make it easier for a rider to sit in the saddle at the lope and to go with the gentle motion of the horse.

The rider must not be tempted, when riding at the jog or lope, to hang on to the reins or horn in order to maintain his seat. If the reins are hung on to the horse's mouth will be hurt, and by hanging on to the horn, the rider will pull himself out of the saddle, and it will take longer to establish a good deep seat. However, in the case of an emergency or uncertainty, when a lifeline is needed, it is far better to hold the horn than to grab the reins.

CHANGING THE PACE   To bring a horse down from one pace to another apply an even pressure with the legs and then take up a light contact with the reins. If the horse does not respond at once, he must be asked again until he does respond, relaxing hand and leg pressure in between each request. Continuous pulling will result in the horse fighting the request.

The Aids

All aids should be given quietly, clearly and firmly to ensure that the horse understands the request. A common error with novice riders is one of confusing the horse by giving contradictory instructions. For example, many people urge the horse forward with the legs while hanging on to his mouth. Consequently, the horse has no idea whether he is supposed to move forwards, backwards or stand still.

Once the horse responds to an instruction and maintains the pace required, the hands and legs must be relaxed, repeating the request only if it is required. Perpetual kicking with the legs and nagging with the hands will establish a situation where the horse soon learns to ignore all requests completely.

Control

Ideally the basics of riding should be taught in an enclosed school where the rider can progress steadily and with confidence, but all too often riders spend *all* their time in the school, never having the chance to ride out and to learn how to control a horse in the open. For example, during the two and a half years I helped to run a Western riding stable in Spain, several people rode with me who were, seemingly, experienced riders, but when confronted with fenceless open country, suddenly lost confidence in their own ability to control the horse. Their confidence was restored once they realised that, when asked to jog or lope, the horses did not bolt into the sierras with them, and also stopped when asked.

Lack of open riding land available to riders in Britain can be a problem as can the busy roads that often have to be crossed to get to open spaces, but every rider should take any opportunity offered to ride out.

Schooling is essential to acquire technical proficiency, showing can be fun and provides a stage for riders to demonstrate their own and their horse's, skills, but can a rider call his knowledge complete if he lacks the confidence to apply his technical proficiency to controlling a horse in open country? After all, is not the company of a good horse in attractive surroundings one of the most pleasurable aspects of riding?

Converting the 'English' rider

Getting the English schooled rider to ride Western is not always quite such an easy task as converting the English horse! Many riders feel that there is a lack of skill to Western riding and that people ride Western because they cannot ride English in the Classical style. Nothing could be further from the truth, as I hope the previous chapters have proved.

At the beginning of this chapter I said that people who rode English could get used to riding Western in a comparatively short time. This is so, but, just as it takes a little time for a horse to be converted, or re-schooled, it takes a little time for an English rider to get used to one or two things.

The most common problems riders face when riding Western for the first time are the longer stirrups, the feel of a Western saddle, maintaining a lighter contact with the horse's mouth and sitting to the jog.

The first and last problems on the above list are easily overcome with practise. Most riders are familiar with working without stirrups to deepen the seat, lengthen the leg and perfect the sitting trot; this exercise can apply equally well to Western riding.

The extra bulk in the structure of a Western saddle can give riders the feeling that they are a long way away from the horse. This, more often than not, is simply a case of just getting used to the feel of the saddle and, again, deepening the seat and lengthening the leg so that the rider is 'drawn' down into the saddle and closer to the horse.

Maintaining a lighter contact with the horse's mouth is one problem that many English riders have trouble with at first, but I have seen a young rider who hung on to a horse's mouth with heavy hands, lighten-up considerably after a few Western riding lessons. She learned how to 'let go' of the horse's head, and her seat and balance also improved because she stopped pulling herself forward by the hands. This general improvement would have been an asset to her future riding, whether riding Western or English.

A good guide to follow when using a shanked Western bit is that, when the bit is *not* being employed, the shanks should point straight down; if the shanks are angled backwards pressure is being applied to the mouth. If this bit position can be maintained without the hand and arm position changing, then the contact should be correct.

6 Western Clothing

As with all things Western, the clothing evolved to suit the job to be done and was influenced by many sources. A New Jersey businessman, a Californian canvas tenting salesman and, of course, the Spanish, via the Mexican vaqueros (S. Am. Sp. = cowboys; Am. = Buckeroo) all played their parts in the metamorphosis of Western riding clothing.

Styles have changed little over the years, but have become more stylised for the show ring, and there is a much wider range of materials, designs and colours to choose from. In recent years Western gear has become popular as fashion and leisure wear, but when choosing clothes for riding, comfort, safety and durability are of paramount importance. Care must be taken to ensure that the items are well made and not just fashionable replicas of good working clothes. Always buy the best (which is not necessarily the most expensive or fancy) that can be afforded. Good Western gear is available in England, but shop around!

The Western hat and high-heeled boots are probably the best known trade marks of the Western rider.

The Hat

Whilst the hat is still expected to perform its basic duties of sunshade and umbrella, it may not now be called upon to double as drinking vessel for man and horse and bucket or campfire fanner, as were its ancestors.

After the American Civil War, with the onset of the big northbound cattle drives, the war veterans turned cowboy wore any hat they could get their hands on. During the war, in the early 1860s, John Batterson Stetson went west to improve his

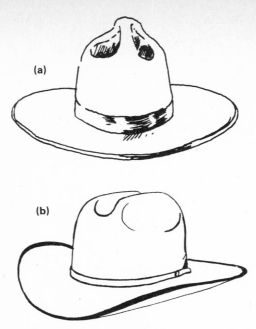

Hats: *(above)* an old-style hat with a 'Montana peak' crease; *(below)* the modern Western hat

health and saw a need for a specialised hat to suit the rigorous lifestyle of the men in the youthful cattle industry. He returned east in 1865, set up shop in Philadelphia and made hats for the Western trade. Within a few years 'Stetson' and 'John B' became synonymous with Western headgear.

The cost of a Stetson could be $20–$30 or more, a princely sum for a man whose average pay was $30 a month, but the hat, like the boots, was considered a lifetime's investment. The finest, and most expensive, of Stetson's hats were made from Beaver felt, a material guaranteed to hold its style and shape for many years, no matter how it was treated!

Modern hat manufacturers often introduce new styles in a variety of colours to cater for personal preference or to match showing outfits, and a recent innovation, the straw Stetson, has become popular with people working in warmer climates and in the show ring.

A cowboy took a great deal of pride in his work; riding and roping were considered to be respectable jobs and a cut above farm labouring. This attitude was reflected in a cowboy's hand and footwear.

Gloves

Leather gloves were worn, not only to protect the hands from rope burns and for warmth, but to protect the hands for the cowboy's higher calling; his hands would not have been as calloused as those of a farmworker!

Boots

Cowboys would never have worn shoes or the thick-soled boots favoured by farmworkers. A cowboy's boots were made for riding not walking and had thin soles through which the stirrups could be felt. Fine leather was used for the uppers to give a glove-like fit. A good pair of made-to-measure boots could cost the same as a hat: about $20–$30.

In the early days of the West the boot legs were not usually shorter than 44 cm (17½ in), straight-legged, undecorated and, for ease of pulling on, had leather straps, known as 'mule-ears', sewn to either the inside or the outside of the boot tops.

A shorter boot, called a 'pee-wee', was not popular because, when the foot was in the stirrup and the heel pushed down, the top of the boot came below the hem of the pant legs (Western trousers were, and are, usually known as pants), and bits of grit, brush and rocks found their way into the boots. At this time all boot heels were fairly flat and the boot toes were square or rounded.

As time went by boot tops widened (to allow air to circulate), but stayed fairly long, heels grew higher and more sloped and boots were often stitched, not only for decoration, but to reinforce the leather and to stop the boot tops collapsing with wear. The toes became more pointed for ease of picking up a stirrup quickly and the higher heels enabled a cowboy to push his feet home in the stirrup (i.e. the stirrup rests against the heel of the boot under the instep) without fear of the foot going right through the stirrup. This was less tiring than riding with the

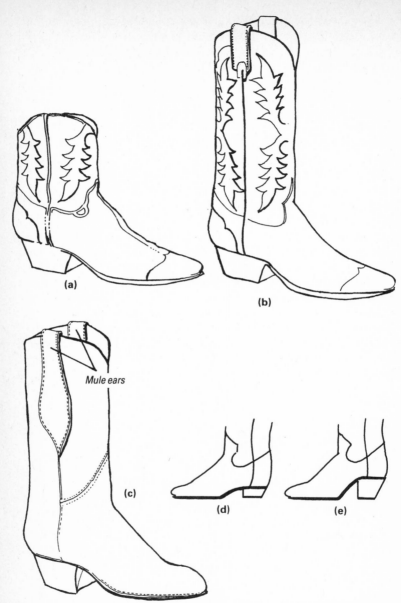

Boots: **(a)** The modern Western boot; **(b)** the short 'pee wee' boot; **(c)** an old-style Western boot with 'mule-ears'; **(d)** walking heel; **(e)** riding heel

stirrup under the ball of the foot when spending long hours in the saddle. To this end a good Western boot had, and should still have, a steel shank under the arch (instep) to strengthen the boot and stop it from giving in the middle under strain. Boots were also put under strain when the cowboy roped from the ground. The high, sloped heels were dug into the ground to act as brakes against the weight of the animal on the other end of the rope.

When buying boots for riding, check to see that they are well made and that they have the steel shank under the arch. Fashion boots do not have the shank and their heels may be hollow which not only makes them weak, but also impossible to repair. If, whilst on this inspection tour, it is revealed that the boots have man-made soles and heel caps, this does not necessarily indicate a lower standard of boot. Many modern boot manufacturers are using man-made materials as they are longer-lasting and cheaper to repair than leather. However, for comfort, the uppers should be leather.

There is no reason why boots worn for everyday riding cannot be worn in the show ring, provided they are clean! The fancy coloured and patent leather boots will not win any more prizes than the plainer working boots. The heel height and shape and the toe shape should be chosen in accordance with personal preference and comfort.

Chaps

Chaps (Mex. = *chaparejos* or *chaparreras*) are leather overalls – in English pronounced 'shaps'. These Western leggings were worn for protection against brush country, cow horns and cold. They were also added protection should a cowboy get thrown, fallen on or stomped on by horse or cow. The modern working cowboy still wears the heavy leather chaps of his forefathers, but modern rodeo and show chaps are made of a finer leather, are often decorated and personalised, or coloured to match an outfit, but they do not afford a great deal of protection.

There are three styles of chaps; chinks, shotgun and batwing.

CHINKS Handed down from the Mexicans, all chaps developed from the armitas (Sp. *amar* = to arm) or chinks (C. A.

Chaps and a show outfit: **(a)** shotgun chaps; **(b)** chinks; **(c)** a girl's show outfit; **(d)** rear view of batwing chaps; **(e)** woollies

Sp. *chingaderos* and *chingar* = to dock, cut off). These were two apron-like leg coverings fastened at the waist and knees with thongs, and coming only to the knees. They were favoured in light brush country and were cooler in hot climates. Many riders in the hot south-west still prefer them.

All chaps are joined at the front by a thin thong which snaps easily should a rider get hung up on the saddle horn, and are fastened at the back or side by a buckled strap.

SHOTGUN   The first Texan derivation of the Mexican chaparejos were the 'shotgun' chaps. These were pulled on like trousers (pants) over the boots, and spurs had to be taken off before putting the chaps on or taking them off. These 'shotguns' often had fringeing running the length of the leg which, as well as being decorative, encouraged the water to run off the chaps in wet weather. Each leg of these chaps had one seam which was sewn in such a way that they looked like the twin barrels of a shotgun, hence the name.

In the north 'hair pants' or chaps made from hides with the hair left on the outside were quite popular. They were warm, but in wet weather the hair or wool absorbed the rain and held it which made the chaps uncomfortably heavy and smelly! They were also known as Angoras or Woollies because they were made from the hides of Angora goats.

BATWING   The most popular chaps were the heavy bullhide batwing chaps, which, as the name suggests, were wide flapping leg pieces fastened with snaps. It was, therefore, no problem to put them on or take them off even with spurs on.

When Western riding made its first appearance in the show ring, the humble cotton shirts and blue denim jeans began to take a back seat.

Shirts and Bandanas

The cowboys' wool or cotton shirts were generally collarless and in drab colours; dark colours did not reflect sunlight and cause glare. The back of the neck was protected by a neckerchief or bandana (from the Hindi *bandhnu*, via the eastern United States). This large square of cotton or silk was folded corner to corner and tied either at the front or back of the neck. It was also called upon to be a towel, handkerchief, sling, tourniquet, horse hobbles, a strainer of muddy water, and to protect the face from dust, sand and ice in storms.

Shirts became brighter when new dyes and materials became available (the anti-glare campaign was handed over to sunglasses!) and, today, Western shirts come in every colour imaginable, plain or patterned, as well as the perennially popular checked designs. The smaller thinner neckerchiefs and bolo ties are now more popular than the very large bandanas in the show ring. The bolo tie in particular gives a neat, finished look to a show outfit as it is a very thin tie of leather or twisted nylon cord, fastened at the neck by a decorative buckle.

Jeans and Riding Pants

Jeans and the new riding pants, many in stretch materials, also became available in a number of colours, stripes and checks, and there is a choice of cut to the leg; straight, slightly flared or boot cut. The latter are cut low over the heel so that when seated in the saddle, the jeans still sit low on the heel and not halfway up the boot. Similarly some show chaps are cut very low over the heel to give emphasis to the downward angle of the heel when the foot is in the stirrup.

More recently, the Western Equitation suit has become very popular in the show ring, particularly with girls. This consists of matching, or colour co-ordinated, riding pants, jacket and/or waistcoat and shirt in a colour of the rider's choice. The hat, and chaps if worn, may also match the rest of the outfit.

Although it is easy to think of the blue denim jeans as the working pants that have been around for a long time, they too were once the new-fangled pants.

Prior to 1850, and the arrival of Levi Strauss from the east, it was (as with the hat in pre-Stetson days) a case of making do with whatever pants were available. Levi Strauss arrived in San Francisco with a load of canvas cloth he hoped to sell for tenting in the mining camps, but he discovered a greater need for tough working clothes. He made his canvas into pants which were an overnight success in the camps. Strauss started a factory at 98 Battery Street, San Francisco, where the company remains to this day, and the popularity of 'Levi's' pants spread to the ranching community. Strauss switched from canvas to the heavyweight cotton material, denim, which was named after the town of its manufacture in France; the material was the serge de Nimes. He then added copper rivets at all the stress points for greater durability.

Up until the 1890s most Westerners wore their pants tucked into their boots, but when decorated boots came into being, they started to wear their pants outside the boots, perhaps because they were either embarrassed by the 'fancy bits' and wished to cover them up, or because they liked them and wished to protect them from wear. At about this time, however, cowboys were becoming ranch hands with more chores than just trail riding, and by wearing the pants outside the boots the bottoms could be turned back to make handy receptacies for holding nails and staples when mending fences etc.

It was also inconvenient to carry anything in the pockets of the pants as it would prove bulky when in the saddle and difficult to get anything out of the pockets, so a vest (waistcoat) was often worn to carry small items of equipment.

Belts

The cowboy rarely used suspenders (braces) to support his pants as they chafed and hindered freedom of movement when working. Belts were also a rarity, usually worn only to show off a rodeo prize buckle. Pants were bought to fit and stay up of their own accord.

Belts are now an accepted part of Western dress, worn as a smart and decorative addition to an outfit, particularly in the show ring where it adds a neat and finished look. Western leather belts can be plain, carved, tooled or stitched, or a combination of all these, and the buckles, which come in a multitude of sizes and designs and are made in materials which range from leather to silver and gold, are often awarded as prizes at shows and rodeos. Despite their decorative quality, Western belts are also quite capable of holding up jeans should they be required to do so!

Outfits for the Show Ring

Show outfits should be neat, clean and practical. Show rules may not specify what sort of outfits should be worn in classes, but it is taken as read that Western hats and boots are to be worn in all classes. Chaps, spurs and gloves, however, are optional, and, when worn, gloves should be leather not string.

In showing classes such as Halter classes, Western Pleasure and Western Equitation, equitation suits are often favoured, although not obligatory, but the outfits should, perhaps, be a little more formal than for the Trail Class, Stock Horse Class and Western games, where I prefer to see a smart but more workmanlike outfit of Western shirt and jeans. In Britain we cannot rely on the weather so it is always advisable to have a Western jacket on hand to avoid freezing in the ring.

Pleasure and Trail Riding Outfits

When following these pursuits it is most important that jeans, shirts and jackets fit well and are comfortable, and wet weather gear should never be far from the back of the saddle. The Western raincoat, the slicker, covers rider, saddle and a great deal of the horse, and is an invaluable item of clothing.

When buying boots please take into consideration that which the cowboy did not, the fact that you may have to walk in them! On long trail rides, dismounting and leading a horse for short periods gives him a break, and if he goes lame you may have a long walk home.

As previously mentioned, Western clothes are available in Britain from Western shops and stockists, but should you wish to have anything custom made (such as chaps) there are a number of people contacted through Western Associations and clubs, Western outfitters and some riding magazines, who will make made-to-measure items for you.

7 Western Riding in Britain

Western riding is alive and well in Britain although the uninitiated may have trouble finding it. It has been popular for many years, mainly with individuals or groups of individuals, and despite the fact that there is certainly not a Western riding establishment in every corner of Britain, there may well be a Western riding enthusiast lurking there!

It has been a hard struggle for Western riders to be taken seriously in Britain; 'playing cowboys' is a common jibe from the Westerners' critics. Many riders turned to Western riding either as an additional equine interest, or because, for them, the English style lacked a certain something; and others chose Western riding, once they discovered it, because it offered an alternative to the English style which may never have attracted them.

Whatever the reason for the initial inspiration, the early Western riders soon realised that they were a little in the dark and had to search for books to increase their knowledge and seek out like-minded people with whom to discuss their problems, ideas and discoveries.

Associations

In 1968 a group of these enthusiasts got together and formed the Western Horsemen's Association of Great Britain 'to provide a representative body for all interested in the Western style of riding and to set and maintain a higher standard of horsemanship and turnout'. The W.H.A. is affiliated to the British Horse Society, and organises shows, events, instructional clinics, trail rides etc., for its members. There is also a series of riding examinations which may be taken, culminating in the Instructor's Certificate.

The W.H.A. secretary is Mr Colin Ward, 36 Old Fold View, Arkley, Barnet, Herts., EN5 4EB.

There are two other Western Associations that cater for Western riding to a varying degree.

The British Westerners' Association caters for all interests in the West including Western Riding, and believes that an understanding of the history of this form of riding is an asset when learning to ride Western. For further details contact the B.W.A. Secretary, Mrs Jacqui Groom, 44 Cainhoe Road, Clophill, Bedfordshire.

The Western Equitation Society is the most recently formed group and caters solely for those interested, as the name suggests, in Western equitation. Their show events do not include Western games such as Barrel Racing. For further details contact the W.E.S. Secretary, Mrs Barbara Carder, 65 Wealdbridge Road, North Weald, Epping, Essex, CM16 6ES.

There are a number of shows in Britain where riders may participate in Western events, and our versatile British Western mounts will be seen taking part in everything from Cattle Cutting to a Western Pleasure class, and from the quiet formality of a Reining Class to the fun and speed of Barrel Racing.

Roping is one event that will not be seen in Britain as it is in North America, because it is frowned upon by animal protection societies, but Break-Away Roping has been tried. This is where a light string hitch is attached to the rope, and, once the animal is roped, the hitch breaks with the weight of the animal pulling against it.

Western Riding Events

WESTERN PLEASURE CLASS In this event the horse is being judged. He must show that he is a pleasure to ride at all paces and is judged on manners, performance, conformation and suitability to the rider.

WESTERN HORSEMANSHIP OR EQUITATION CLASS In this event the rider is judged. The rider should have a good seat, hands and leg position, and is judged on his ability to apply the aids correctly to get his horse to perform certain movements.

TRAIL CLASS   The horse is required to negotiate various objects and problems, both ridden and led, that simulate things he may have to cope with on the trail, e.g. picking his way over and around objects, standing while his rider opens and shuts a gate, jumping a small fence, backing round right-angled turns, dragging an object behind him, walking through water etc. He will be judged on his ability to carry out all tests calmly and willingly, and on how well he moves at the walk, trot and lope.

REINING PATTERN CLASSES   The horse must perform set movements. The horse is required to follow a set test, not unlike a dressage test, and is judged on his ability to perform the set movements, responding to the rein, leg and body cues (aids) of his rider.

STOCK HORSE CLASS   The horse is judged on his ability to work cattle and has to demonstrate skills related to stock work such as ground-tying and rope work.

CATTLE CUTTING   There are some shows in Britain where Cattle Cutting contests are held. The horse has to cut a particular animal out from a group of cattle, and keep the animal away from its chums for a set amount of time.

Other Events

Western shows also run the popular gymkhana-style events, two of the most popular of which are Barrel Racing and Pole Bending.

BARREL RACING   This is a timed event which is run around three barrels in a cloverleaf pattern. Horse and rider must go round the barrels in a set way, and the fastest over the finishing line wins. Barrel racing is a popular event with girls, and is one where skill as well as speed is required; a good barrel horse must rein well.

POLE BENDING   Horse and rider must 'bend' back and forth through a line of upright poles, and, again, the fastest competitor over the finishing line wins.

VERSATILITY   In the Versatility class the horse must work equally well in both the Western and English styles. Both horse and rider must be correctly attired for both styles of riding. The horse is judged first under Western tack then, after a quick change, under English tack.

SHOWMANSHIP   The rider is judged on his ability to show his horse, in halter, to its best advantage. Both horse and rider must be well turned-out.

Trail Riding or Long Distance Riding

This is a sport that has many devotees amongst Western riders, and it is becoming increasingly popular in Britain. It is one where the horses have to be supremely fit and can demonstrate their stamina and agility covering trails, which are sometimes very rough, in a good time. There are three categories of trail riding: Pleasure, Competitive and Endurance.

THE PLEASURE RIDE   The one non-competitive ride; it is organised to give riders a good day out in the country.

Competitive and Endurance

These are competitive, cover more ground than the Pleasure rides (sometimes 2 or 3 days), and the riders are judged on their ability to get home within the time limit with their horses sound and in good condition. The horses have regular veterinary checks throughout the longer rides to ensure they are fit enough to continue.

American Horse Breeds in Britain

It has already been stated that most breeds make good Western mounts, but for those who wish to choose a breed of horse closer to the roots of Western riding, there are some American breeds that have established themselves on British soil. They include the Quarter Horse, the Appaloosa and the Morgan Horse, all three of which have their own Associations.

THE BRITISH QUARTER HORSE ASSOCIATION Quarter Horses have been trickling into Britain since the 1960s, and now many 'homebred' purebreds are registered both in the British Quarter Horse Registry and the American Quarter Horse Registry. The British Quarter Horse Association was founded in 1974 and has its own stallion list and stud book. For further details and membership information contact the Secretary, Mrs Patricia Dyke, The Mill House, Lubenham, Market Harborough, Leicestershire.

THE BRITISH APPALOOSA SOCIETY The Appaloosa, best known for its strikingly spotted coat, is another breed which is extremely worthy of the title 'Western horse'. It was the first horse breed to be selectively bred by a North American Indian tribe, the Nez Perce Indians of the Palouse country in Idaho.

The British Appaloosa Society was formed in 1976 when the British Spotted Horse & Pony Society was dissolved. For full details and membership information contact the Secretary, Mrs D. de Rivaz, Ash Cottage, Icomb, Stow-on-the-Wold, Gloucestershire.

THE BRITISH MORGAN HORSE SOCIETY The Morgan Horse is not usually thought of as a Western mount, but has proved himself to be a very able stock horse, favoured by many in America. This small, compact and agile breed was started by just one stallion, Justin Morgan, in the 1780s, and was founded in Britain in 1975 when the breed made its first British home in Ross-on-Wye in Herefordshire. For full details and membership information contact Mrs A. Conner Bulmer, George & Dragon Hall, Mary Place, London, W11.

All three of these societies hold their own Annual Breed Show.

Once again versatility is a trait shared by the above breeds who have proved their worth not only in the Western field, but are equally at home under stock saddle, dressage saddle, jumping saddle and in harness.

Glossary of Western Terms

A LA BRIDA	A riding style the Spaniards learned from the Christian crusaders in the Holy Land who rode with a very long stirrup and used a heavily padded saddle with a high pommel and cantle.
A LA GINETA	A riding style the Spaniards learned from the Saracens who rode with very short stirrups and stood in the stirrups when riding at speed.
ARMITAS	(See Chaps.)
BANDANA	The large multi-purpose neckerchief worn by cowboys.
BOSAL	The original Spanish hackamore or bitless bridle.
BUCKEROO	An American word for cowboy. (See Vaquero.)
CENTRE FIRE	(See Rigging Positions.) Rim fire and centre fire. The only definitions of these terms I have come across are those in *Western Horse Behaviour and Training* by Robert W. Miller (published by Doubleday Dolphin). Mr Miller states: '. . . You might be interested in the origin of the terms center fire and rim fire. It comes from rifle cartridges, some of which are fired when the firing pin of the gun hits the center of the cartridge. Another type fires when the pin hits the explosive cap on the edge or rim of the cartridge.' A classic example of how words

in the Western vocabulary have been adopted and adapted!

CHAPS The protective leather leggings worn by the cowboy and Western rider. Types: Armitas or chinks, knee length or just below knee length chaps. Shotgun, narrow-legged full length chaps. Batwing, wide-legged, full length chaps.

CHEYENNE ROLL The additional piece of leather at the rear of some saddle cantles.

CINCH The Western girth.

CONQUISTADORES The Spanish conquerors of America whose riding style and equipment became those of the cowboy and Western rider.

COW (OR STOCK) HORSE The horse trained to work cattle or stock.

COW SAVVY The cow horse's knowledge of how a cow thinks and moves.

CRICKET (See Roller.)

CURB BIT A curb bit has a leverage action, i.e. the action on the mouth comes via the shanks and not directly on to the mouth as with the snaffle bits.

CURB STRAP (OR CHAIN) Attaches to the shanks above the mouthpiece of the curb bit, and when the reins are pulled, applies pressure into the curb (chin) groove.

CUTTING HORSE The cow horse that is used to cut cattle from the herd.

CUTTING SADDLE The saddle that has a fork with wide swells extending on either side of the pommel which help anchor the rider into the saddle.

DALLY To wrap the rope around the saddle horn when roping as opposed to tying it.

FENDER (Also known as *sudadero*.) The wide piece of leather that covers the stirrup leather and protects the rider's leg from the horse's sweat.

FIADOR (Also known as *Theadore*.) A throatlash

74

made of fine rope, rawhide or cotton, used to keep the bosal in place. The fiador is tied in intricate and decorative knots and fastened to the heel knot of the bosal. It is not always used as it can restrict the movement of the bosal.

FLANK CINCH   The rear cinch used to prevent a roping saddle tipping up.

FORK   The front arch of the saddle tree.

GROUND-TYING   Ensuring a horse stands still when one, or both, of his reins are dropped to the ground. He must learn to be 'tied to the ground'.

HACKAMORE   The bitless bridle. Types: The bosal or the mechanical hackamore.

HALF-BREED BIT   A curb bit which is a modification of the Spade bit. It has about half the port height of the Spade.

HORN   The object on top of the saddle fork around which the rope is dallied or tied when roping.

IN-SKIRT RIGGING   (See Rigging.)

JOG   The slow Western trot.

LATIGO   The leather strap that secures the cinch by tying or buckling.

LOPE   The slow Western canter.

MECATE   (Also known as McCarty.) The hair rope used for the reins of the bosal.

MUSTANG   The feral horse of the American plains; the first cow pony.

NECK-REINING   The art of turning the horse with both reins in one hand.

ONE-EAR BRIDLE   (Also known as Split-ear bridle.) These bridles are kept on the horse's head by means of a leather loop or split in the leather of the crown piece, through which one of the horse's ears is pulled.

ON-TREE RIGGING   (See Rigging.)

PORT   The arch in the centre of the mouthpiece of a curb bit. Ports may be high, medium or low.

QUIRT	The Western whip.
REATA	The rawhide rope.
RIGGING	That which, combined with the cinch, keeps the saddle in place. Rigging is either on-tree or in-skirt, i.e. the rigging rings are either in the leather rigging straps on the tree, or built into the skirt. Saddles may be single-, with a front cinch only, or double-, with front and flank cinch, rigged.
RIGGING POSITIONS	The different positions in which the rigging rings are placed. The positions are: Spanish (rim-fire or full), $7/8$, $3/4$, $5/8$ and centre-fire.
RIM-FIRE	(See Rigging positions.)
RODEO	Competitions in which cowboys compete to exhibit their skills and those of their stock horses.
ROLLER (OR CRICKET)	A 'toy' placed in the centre of the port of a Spade bit with which the horse can play with his tongue. This helps to quiet the horse and stimulates salivation.
ROMAL	The leather extension on the end of joined reins which can be used as a quirt.
ROPING HORSE	The cow horse used by the man who ropes the cattle.
ROPING SADDLE	This saddle is used to facilitate freedom of movement for the roper. It has very narrow, or no, swells, and often has a higher horn than a cutting saddle. It is a double-rigged saddle.
ROWEL	The free-moving spiked wheel on a Western spur.
SACKING-OUT	A method of training used to make a cow horse as spook-proof as possible.
SHANKS	The metal arms on a curb bit which provide the leverage for control.
SLICKER	The large Western raincoat that covers man, saddle and a large proportion of horse.
SPADE BIT	A curb bit which has a particularly high port.
STOCK SADDLE	The saddle designed for use by the stockman or cowboy; the Western saddle.

STRAIGHT-UP	When a cow horse is finally working well in a curb bit he is said to be straight-up in the bridle.
SWELLS	Wide extensions on either side of the fork of a Western saddle.
TAPADEROS	Leather stirrup covers that protect the feet.
TIE-DOWN	The Western martingale.
VAQUERO	The Mexican cowboy. Some American cowboys are known as Buckeroos, a derivation of vaquero.

Readers of this book who wish to be informed about new and forthcoming publications on horses and horsemanship are invited to send their names and addresses to:

J. A. ALLEN & CO. LTD.,
1, Lower Grosvenor Place,
Buckingham Palace Road,
London, SW1W 0EL